The NEWCOMER'S DICTIONARY

D1601629

The
NEWCOMER'S
DICTIONARY

JOYCE AGEE
Illustrated by Ellen Agee

Springtime **Books**
Bringing Your Book to Life

First published in Great Britain by Springtime Books

ISBN: 978-1-9196133-3-8

Illustrated by Ellen Agee Rehfuss
Edited, designed and typeset by Caz Brown
Cover photograph courtesy Agee family
Author photograph by Richard Shaw
Map of Gallipolis courtesy Sewah Studios, Marrietta, Ohio

This book is dedicated to our mother Betty,
who nurtured our love of beauty.

acknowledgements

To my sister Ellen — time-travelling companion, who listened, aided, abetted and edited while I charted our past; who recalled details I had forgotten; and whose collage illustrations so expressively capture the surreal quality of our childhood.

To my husband Greg Pearce, a loving and patient central pillar; and to our extended family who keep the home fires burning: Regan Pearce and her partner Matt Drew and their son Huxley, Kris Holman and Hugh Lowey; and to Greg's son and family who provided lodging upon our return to Australia. To long-time friends in Melbourne, Josephine Dyer, Anne-Marie Cooper and Jacqueline Taylor who weren't always sure how to help upon our return but still tried repeatedly with meals, professional introductions and encouragement. Author Ken Brandt and designer and artist Judy Brandt who gave much appreciated advice and guidance. Special thanks to Cheryl Cromer for her years of encouragement. David Hoffman who has never let distance and change interfere with the quality of our enduring friendship.

And to those who graciously helped to smooth the departure from Seattle, Washington, Dave Ghosal and Trudz Pearce; and special thanks to those who consoled and advised us during the difficult re-entry back to Australia, especially Julie Highton and Ryan Stutt. Sumalee Oakley, military brat, who sparked the initial idea for the dictionary with our discussion about the word 'transfer'.

A wistful thanks to all those from our past who disappeared, but whom we still recall with affection: to my first-grade friend red-headed Pam Bowers in Alabama and, on my sister's behalf, to Jamie in Richmond, Virginia, and her friend

acknowledgements

Susan Johnson in Pennsylvania. We disappeared and never had the opportunity to say how much you mattered to us.

I would like to acknowledge the West Gippsland Regional Libraries and the staff of the Warragul Public Library who ensured that the many necessary books were available despite the challenges of COVID-19 restrictions; Librarian Morag Stewart at the University of Washington Libraries in Seattle, Washington, who used her considerable skills to locate the origin of a quote, and Colin Walker from the Bodleian Library in Oxford who responded promptly to my questions, traversing time, distance and literature. Libraries and librarians are a continuous wonder.

My grateful appreciation to Caz Brown, capable and diligent editor and thoughtful designer, who brought insight, patience and understanding to this enterprise during the time of COVID. At the time of writing this, I would not recognise her if we met on the street. It has been a trip!

Joyce Agee
January 2022

contents

introduction

Professional Newcomers are people who move home frequently as a result of work or personal circumstances. I have outstanding qualifications in this field. My mother Betty used the term to describe us when she was introduced to people for the first time. Most people will find themselves a newcomer at some point: starting a job; going to a new school; joining a club or organisation; or moving to a new location. Being a frequent newcomer can bring complex challenges.

From the late 1950s to the early '70s, our nuclear family moved home seven times up and down the eastern seaboard of the United States. Our father, Thomas 'Tom' Agee, was a mechanical engineer, who worked for corporate America. He contributed to the design of special projects, ranging from a space rocket to golf clubs. Whenever he was assigned to a new project, we transferred to a new state. As a consequence, my sister Ellen and I attended seven different public schools in six different states before reaching the age of seventeen.

Our first transfer was from Ohio to Florence, Alabama, where we moved into a small rental house on a quiet suburban street. Mother tried to finish her university degree and, at the same time, took the opportunity to separate from our father for six months. We moved to Louisville, Kentucky, where my sister and I were enrolled at a new school in the middle of the academic year. Eventually, our parents reconciled and we returned to Alabama before being transferred to Virginia.

Our moves taught us that conforming to local dress codes and having an indistinguishable accent were key to personal survival in a new place. Moving forced us to adapt. We had to figure out the new social hierarchy and how to fit in. As

introduction

perennial outsiders, we had no understanding of how people related to each other, whether as friends or family. Neither did we know how to develop lasting relationships that would enable us to belong.

Though still young, we were forced to address fundamental issues of identity, self-worth, connection and belonging. This experience shaped our lifelong attitudes, expectations and behaviour. Eventually, as young adults, we figured out that predictable biennial transfers afforded us a unique opportunity to reinvent ourselves, leaving behind aspects of our personality that we didn't like.

The newcomer impulse escalated after I left home, eventually reaching an international scale. I moved another eight times, including a stint in England, a move to Sydney, Australia, and a ten-year period in Seattle, Washington, with my husband and stepdaughter. Moving had become an ingrained habit as well as a way of avoiding personal problems. I pursued a career as a freelance photographer and, later, worked in the arts and cultural sector as a curator, a project manager in community museums and local government and in libraries development.

My husband and I moved back to Melbourne, Australia, in 2015 and It was during this lonely and uncertain period that I began to write *The Newcomer's Dictionary*, exploring words, ideas and the complicated feelings I faced being new once again.

This move proved more difficult than either of us could have imagined. We had assumed that being in familiar places with friends and family would make the transition easier.

introduction

Finding work was particularly challenging. My steady employment history at the University of Washington Libraries, with a proven track record and good references, was hardly recognised. Suddenly, I felt invisible again. Whatever I had accomplished before was of little consequence. It took nearly a year of constant networking and countless rejections before I was finally offered the role of senior curator and collections manager at a community museum in Melbourne.

Each dictionary entry contains a deeper question: How do we feel about being new? How do we maintain a sense of equilibrium when everything around us is changing? How do we manage change without losing sight of who we are? What do we really care about? Who genuinely cares about us? How can we deal with our emotions if we feel rejected by the 'settled' people?

In a number of entries I refer to relevant books, plays and films that made an impression on me, either growing up or as an adult. Books and films became my sanctuary from constant change. In the world of fiction, my sister and I were able to immerse ourselves in deeper and richer expressions of feelings.

Many of the entries talk about the challenges of being a serial newcomer, but this book is also about language and the way words and stories can help bring us closer to ourselves and others. When words aren't enough, the accompanying illustrations created by my sister Ellen eloquently capture our childhood's transient feelings.

Whether you identify as a serial newcomer or are in the midst of a minor move, I hope this collection of words and

introduction

illustrations will bring clarity and reassurance, help to anchor your feelings and, in time, become a valued keepsake.

Moving will always bring unexpected obstacles, but dealing with these and adjusting quickly is what makes for a stable transition. At one point, I was seeing a counsellor and telling her about my background and frequent moves, delivering an upbeat version of my itinerant life with animated highlights. After I finished, she looked at me and quietly asked, 'Now, how do you really feel?' No one had ever asked me that question before.

Joyce Agee
January 2022

A

abroad

adverb in or to a foreign
country or countries;
moving about

noun (collective) foreign countries

abroad

Drop the word 'abroad' into a conversation and it can sound either mildly charming or oddly stilted. Mention having lived, studied or toured abroad and suddenly there is a vague aroma of violet-scented sachets mingled with the scent of old-fashioned societal privilege.

My sister and I attended a private women's college in the southern United States where 'abroad' was common parlance. This small school offered a study-abroad programme through which selected students lived and attended classes in Paris or London. These overseas junkets were jokingly referred to as 'the colonials' efforts to make up for four hundred years' lack of culture.'

In the past, the capacity to travel abroad and tour the European continent or other fashionable places was evidence of personal or familial wealth. Travelling abroad or undertaking the 'Grand Tour', as it was more commonly known, was social code for the snobbish pursuit of cultural polish in lieu of the necessity to earn a living. This cultural divide shows up in Margaret Mitchell's novel *Gone with the Wind* (1936), in which the Tarletan twins realise that being expelled from college will blight any chance of an overseas tour, bankrolled by their mother. As if this weren't enough, the American Civil War and the abolition of slavery would also inconveniently intervene. Author Henry James explored the cultural divide between upper crust Americans and Europeans in his novels *The American* (1877) and *The Ambassadors* (1903).

Not everyone ventures abroad for the same reason. The experience of our family's Protestant Huguenot forebears would have been vastly different from these cultural forays. In the

A

18th century, after enduring religious persecution and receiving death threats, this plucky group migrated from France to the United States. We can only imagine the deep emotions associated with such an upheaval.

The use of travel as a measure of cultural worth and social standing has waned, which might explain the decline in the use of 'abroad'. With the rise of online chats and streaming services, it is no longer necessary to physically travel to go abroad.

So does the word 'abroad' have any value in our modern times? For the newcomer, it suggests a distance travelled, freedom of movement and an expanded outlook. Time to throw away the starched crinolines and lace doilies and repurpose 'abroad' to signal that we are moving forward with a deeper understanding of ourselves and others.

There are some things one can only achieve by a deliberate leap in the opposite direction. One has to go abroad in order to find the home one has lost.

— Franz Kafka, author

B
belong

verb 1 to be a member, adherent, inhabitant, etc

2 to have the proper qualifications, especially social qualifications, in order to be a member of a group

3 to be proper or due, be properly or appropriately placed, situated, etc

B

Moving frequently, my sister and I were never certain who was trustworthy or who we could confide in. We felt a strong need to belong yet we were deeply suspicious of belonging. American comedian Groucho Marx (1890–1977) expressed this dilemma when he famously joked, 'I don't want to belong to any club that will accept me as a member.'

As newcomers, we often felt exposed and vulnerable. If someone showed impatience with us or, worse, decided to ignore us, it felt desperate and irreparable. We knew first impressions could make the difference between acceptance or being ostracised.

Despite Groucho's misgivings, joining a club or social group as a newcomer can be worthwhile. As newcomers, my sister and I joined the local Brownies and Girl Scouts, and our mother attended luncheons and other activities sponsored by the Newcomers Club.

As young teenagers in Pennsylvania, our mother enrolled us in dance lessons. My sister remembers the jazz ballet dance teacher intentionally embarrassing her — she felt so uncomfortable that she refused to go again. As for me, I did not show a great aptitude for ballet and my teacher wisely favoured other students.

Groucho's joke was both comic irony and social critique. His family were immigrants of Jewish descent. After his parents married in 1884, they moved to Queens in New York City where he and his brothers were born. Four of the brothers pursued careers as comedians and vaudeville performers. As the Marx Brothers, they progressed successfully into Hollywood films (1920–1940s), and Groucho worked in early

belong

television in the 1950s. Despite their popularity, they experienced anti-Semitism: they were barred from exclusive hotels and denied membership to élite organisations and Groucho's young daughter was prevented from swimming in a pool with friends at a country club that excluded Jews.[1] They were being rejected by the very people Groucho and his brothers entertained.

> Colquet hated reality but realised it was still the only place to get a good steak.
>
> — Woody Allen, film director and scriptwriter
> 'The Condemned'

1   Krebs, A (1977) 'Groucho Marx, comedian, dead; movie star and TV host was 86', *New York Times*, https://www.nytimes.com/1977/08/20/archives/groucho-marx-comedian-dead-movie-star-and-tv-host-was-86-master-of.html, accessed 23 December 2021.

C

castaway

adjective	1	cast adrift; shipwrecked
	2	discarded; thrown away
noun	1	a shipwrecked person
	2	a rejected person or thing

castaway

Once again, we have arrived. The cardboard boxes are unpacked, the adrenalin rush of the physical move is over and we tentatively start to explore our new surroundings. It feels as though we are castaways on a desert island, but without the ocean view.

Castaways in novels and on television offer positive role models for survival during this initial period of uncertainty. *The Swiss Family Robinson* by Johann Wyss (1812) tells the story of a family stranded on a remote island. They thrive, building a sophisticated tree house and planting crops, and eventually they will be rescued. A group of wacky shipwrecked passengers on 'Gilligan's Island', a 1960s American sitcom, seek to replicate the essentials of civilisation — from building a lie detector to a washing machine. Whether from the 19th century or the 1960s, these fictional castaways show ingenuity, a will to survive and interdependence, albeit sometimes reluctantly.

As children, although we couldn't verbalise it, each move made us feel more and more distant from ourselves and others. Externally, the geography changed, but internally, our emotions remained the same. We were perennial strangers marooned on a remote suburban island, wondering whether we would ever be rescued.

I had always felt acutely uncomfortable admitting the toll our childhood took on us until I read about an interview with Hollywood actor Tom Hanks.

Hanks was the guest on the US radio program *Desert Island Discs* in which celebrities name the music and books they would take if cast away. This was no coincidence because he was also promoting his new film, *Cast Away* (2000), about

C

a character who finds himself marooned alone on a Pacific Island. During the program, Hanks suddenly became emotional as he recalled his 'vagabond' childhood and having to move ten times in five years. It was during this difficult time that he decided to become an artist. Despite enormous success, the gruelling memories of an unstable childhood were still painful. His story shows that being a newcomer as a child can have a powerful influence on the direction of our lives.

You'll never leave where you are until you decide where you'd rather be.

— Anonymous

D

disappear

verb	1	become invisible or unnoticeable
	2	become less intense and fade away gradually
	3	lost, as without warning or explanation cease to exist

D

Abracadabra! No magic, mystery or murder. We arrive at our new home and promptly disappear. After a move, regardless of our age or experience, there is an odd sensation of being invisible. Everything that was familiar is altered, routines and rituals are all gone and close friends are missing. For some, the appeal of a move is the chance to make a fresh start, but it can still be a strange period during which we feel adrift, having no clear direction.

As we struggle, there will be individuals who, for inexplicable reasons, want to make the move harder for us.

Returning to Australia after a decade in the US, I responded to an advertisement seeking volunteers at a community museum. The President and a Board member, both elderly, retired men who were also volunteers, arranged to meet with me.

After scanning my résumé, the Board member asked, 'How do I know this is true?'

This was unexpectedly rude, but I knew better than to react and politely replied, 'I have written references and referees who are available by phone or email.'

Then he said, 'We do not like Americans here.'

The other man remained silent. I hold dual citizenship for Australia and America, so why did this complete stranger bully me? This incident was a sad reminder of the spoken and unspoken prejudice experienced by many immigrants, refugees and newcomers after moving to a new country.

As newcomers, we are easy targets. Whatever we have accomplished prior to a move is relegated to history: we must learn to survive with new rules, expectations and biases.

In the end, those who mistreat newcomers are the ones

disappear

who disappear. Our situation is temporary, but their emptiness is permanent.

I learned at an early age to be socially
effective while practising disappearing.
I was always making new friends,
then losing them.

— Sebastian Lelio, filmmaker

E

exile

noun   the state of being barred
from one's native country,
typically for political or
punitive reasons

E

After a major move, everything shifts — not just the furniture, but our feelings, too. The people and things we care about vanish into thin air. It can feel as if we are being sent into exile.

But, if it is any consolation, we are in good company. Mary, Queen of Scots was exiled from Scotland to England after a tumultuous period when, in 1567, she was forced to abdicate in favour of her infant son James VI. In 1814, the French statesman and military leader Napoléon Bonaparte was exiled to the island of Elba after abdicating the throne. This did not discourage his ambitions and he escaped, only to be defeated at the Battle of Waterloo and exiled again in 1815, this time to the island of St Helena.

In Victorian England, homosexuality was considered a crime, so in 1895, after his release from jail, writer Oscar Wilde moved permanently to France. Author Vladimir Nabokov, together with his aristocratic family, escaped the Russian Revolution, fleeing to England. Perhaps the best known contemporary expatriate is the Dalai Lama (b. 1935), Tibet's political leader, who has chosen exile in protest of China's invasion of his country.

I was accustomed to being the perennial newcomer, but it was not until I took a taxi to Sydney airport in Australia that I learned what it feels like to be in exile.

Suddenly, the taxi came to a halt. There was a serious accident ahead and the delay could be more than an hour. With time on our hands, the driver turned off the engine and we rolled down the windows for some warm summer air, scented with exhaust fumes. We began to talk. I asked him about his

exile

background. He looked to be in his early- to mid-thirties. In heavily accented English, he told me that he had been born in China. When the 1989 Tiananmen Square massacre took place in Beijing, he was an international student living in Sydney.

In a humanitarian gesture, the Australian government offered Chinese students sanctuary. Fearing for his safety if he returned to his homeland, he chose exile. At the time, he had been studying medicine but could not get any work in Australia because his main academic qualifications were from China. With an urgent need to earn money, he tried different occupations, from leading groups of Chinese tourists to taxi driving. Did he regret his decision? He admitted it had been difficult to find his place and to be accepted.

He asked me about my background and was very surprised to learn that, as an expatriate American and an Australian citizen, I also had problems finding acceptance and dealing with prejudice: English was my first language and I had light brown hair and hazel eyes, so he assumed that this would prevent many of the problems he had encountered. Startled by the revelation of our shared experience, we looked at each other intently. In the middle of a traffic jam, we had found an unexpected connection and I was given a poignant glimpse into the deeper feelings of someone in exile.

Only the mind cannot be sent into exile.

— Ovid, poet
Epistulae ex Ponto [Letters from the Black Sea]

F

foreign

adjective

1 involving, located in, or coming from another country, area, people, etc; a foreign resident

2 not familiar; strange

3 in an abnormal place or position; foreign matter; foreign bodies

F

At a party held at the Museum of Chinese Australian History, where I was working as the Senior Curator, I was introduced to a young man who was an Australian diplomat. I was immediately intrigued by his career choice of professional foreigner. I learned that his next assignment was in China and asked whether he was looking forward to it.

Clearly accustomed to the question, he replied, 'Yes, I am. And my husband is used to moving ... he was a US "military brat" and always says he felt like a suitcase when he was growing up.' He seemed confident that both he and his husband would have no problem adjusting to a foreign culture or the culture to them.

'Military brat' is slang for a child of military personnel. These families are frequently transferred from one military base to another — one of the few consolations is everyone in that community is in the same situation.

As part of corporate America, our family's experience of moving was somewhat different. Military families are provided with housing, schools and general stores, whereas our parents, before transferring, would have to visit the new area to choose a home, select schools and locate other services. Military families who live on a base can feel foreign together, whereas we could only ever feel foreign alone.

As newcomers, no matter the circumstance, we must adapt — no one will be in a hurry to adjust to us. Moving frequently, the perennial question is: why make any effort if we know we are leaving again?

Foreignness can become embedded in our newcomer psyche. Watchful and wary, we look for behavioural clues to

foreign

gauge whether someone is friend, foe or indifferent. To cope, my sister and I became self-sufficient, which really meant that we grew accustomed to feeling lonely. Fortunately, we had each other and we had books. Ellen became a voracious reader whereas I, having attended four different primary schools in four years, lagged behind.

Fortunately, Mother intervened to help me catch up. Reading became the closest thing we had to a treasured home. In libraries, my sister and I were never foreign: we never had to explain ourselves or fear rejection. In this vast world of ideas and imagination, everything was new but never foreign.

Books were this wonderful escape for me because I could open a book and disappear into it, and that was the only way out of that house when I was a kid.

— Dean Koontz, author

G

gypsy

noun 1   a member of a travelling people traditionally earning a living by itinerant trade and fortune telling

2   informal; a nomad or free-spirited person

gypsy

If you are of Roma heritage, it is a slur to be called a 'gypsy' or the even nastier 'gypo'. Yet, as one of the world's oldest surviving groups of wanderers, like the Bedouins of the Middle East, they survive and thrive to this day.

Centuries ago, their ancestors travelled to Europe from northern India. Today, they speak Romany, a language with roots in Hindi and Punjabi. An astonishing eleven million Roma live and travel in France, Spain, Germany, the United Kingdom, the United States and Australia. Ireland has its own 'travellers', but they have a different ethnicity.[2]

Originally, the Roma worked the land, but as economies shifted they were forced into other occupations such as horse traders, entertainers, dancers or musicians. Along the way, they acquired a dubious reputation for the stereotypical sideline of fortune-telling and gazing into crystal balls.

In some popular novels, the Roma are cast as villains. Vilifying the newcomer is a useful plot device. In Victor Hugo's *The Hunchback of Notre Dame* (1831), Esmeralda, a gypsy entertainer, is doomed to die because of her exceptional beauty, low social standing and unwillingness to conform. Jane Austen depicted gypsies as troublemakers in *Emma* (1815); and Dodie Smith features nefarious dog-snatching gypsies in *The Hundred and One Dalmatians* (1956).

Some people in conservative societies still harbour suspicions of the Roma, but, in their defence, Roma exhibit a remarkable self-reliance and a deep understanding of what it

---

2   North KE, Martin LJ & Crawford MH (2000) 'The origins of the Irish travellers and the genetic structure of Ireland', *Annals of Human Biology*, 27(5):453–65.

G

takes to prosper as permanent outsiders. Practical and practised nomads, they have developed a lifestyle in which everything they value, including family and friends, is portable and can be housed in a caravan.

These close-knit communities, some might say secretive, have a distinct cultural identity and an innate sense of belonging wherever they are, but being a perennial outsider can also be dangerous. During World War II, the Nazis deemed Roma to be racially inferior. It is estimated that more than 250 000 died through malnutrition or disease, or were murdered in the gas chambers.[3]

Today, most newcomers are unlikely to live in a caravan or take up fortune-telling, but this lifestyle offers a powerful model. The Roma do not need a fixed abode for their identity or well-being. Instead, they accept change as inevitable: the strongest predictors for happiness being independence and a lasting pride in their unique history and culture.

> sure, we need gypsies. we always have.
> because if you don't have someone to
> run out of town once in a while, how are you
> going to know you yourself belong there?
>
> — Stephen King, author
> *Thinner*

---

3   United States Holocaust Memorial Museum, Washington DC, 'Documenting numbers of victims of the holocaust and Nazi persecution', https://encyclopedia.ushmm.org/content/en/article/documenting-numbers-of-victims-of-the-holocaust-and-nazi-persecution, accessed 23 December 2021.

H

history

noun   1   the study of past events

2   events of the past

3   past events that relate
to a particular subject,
place, organisation

H

For newcomers who move frequently, our history and memories fragment and scatter behind us like a trail of stale breadcrumbs. In an unwelcome ritual, we leave behind the people and places we value and store our memories away.

Most of our new acquaintances will take no interest in a past they do not share. They might make an exception for a newcomer who falls into the 'prestige' category and who attracts special interest wherever they live.

One such newcomer was the Nobel Prize winner in Physics, Albert Einstein. A German-born Jew, Einstein was 54 years old when he and his second wife Elsa emigrated to the United States after the Nazis came to power in 1933. He was invited to work at Princeton University where he settled in comfortably. He wrote to a friend, 'I hibernate like a bear in its cave, and really feel more at home than ever before in all my varied existence.'

Einstein's achievements over a long and well-publicised career ensured a warm welcome — he would be celebrated wherever he went. But for most serial newcomers, our truncated history, with all its detours and dead ends, is difficult to explain and so we avoid talking about it. But sometimes, as in a fairy tale, our history magically reappears.

As children, my sister and I spent summer vacations with our grandparents on their small farm outside of Gallipolis, Ohio, where our father was born and raised. He is now buried beside our grandparents and a great aunt on a small hillside cemetery on the outskirts of town. During our nomadic childhood, our grandparents, Mamaw and Papaw, were a lifeline, offering continuity and acceptance. Gallipolis became our emotional hometown. Many years later, I returned to Gallipolis for a visit. After going to the cemetery, I decided to walk round the centre of town accompanied by Mother and our stepfather. It was freezing cold and this once thriving town was empty. As we turned a corner, we saw a man in his late sixties — about the age our father would have been had he lived. The man, dressed in a thick coat and scarf, walked briskly towards us. He stopped, smiled and introduced himself. Then he asked us why we were visiting. I introduced myself and mentioned the names of my father and grandparents. Without missing a beat, he said, 'Oh, yes. I remember the Agee family and your grandfather, Thomas Agee Senior.'

Amazed, I felt as though I had dropped into a parallel universe. It had been decades since I had visited Gallipolis yet the first person I met had memories of my family. I was deeply moved. As an adult, I had rarely spoken to anyone outside our immediate family who knew anything about our past. Complicating this, our history had become a liability after both our parents divorced and remarried: no one wanted to revisit the past. At the time, it felt as if my sister and I were being forced to erase another part of ourselves.

Newcomers, whether notable or not, must leave things behind in order to gain the momentum to travel forward. Adapting to change is the only way to survive.

Life is like riding a bicycle. To keep your balance you must keep moving.

— Albert Einstein, physicist

I

itinerant

adjective travelling from place to place

noun a person who travels from place to place

Folk stories serve as reminders of how itinerants can turn the tables on the permanent residents. In the medieval legend, the Pied Piper of Hamelin was hired to deal with the town's rat infestation. When the townspeople reneged on the bargain, he took revenge, luring the village children away with his pipe music.

In another story, 'Stone Soup', hungry itinerants outwit the stingy locals, saying they have a stone that magically will turn water into soup. They drop the stone into a pot of boiling water and then ask for various ingredients, which the intrigued locals supply. Through the art of persuasion, they eventually produce a nutritious stew — enough to feed everyone. Itinerants can be resourceful or dangerous, but the underlying message is 'Beware of strangers'.

Cinematic itinerants are more glamorous. In *Picnic* (1955), a handsome vagabond lures a staid, small town teacher from her predictable life into the romantic unknown. In the film adaptation of John Steinbeck's book *The Grapes of Wrath* (1939), a loving family, displaced from their Midwest farm in the Great Depression, become itinerant, but remain stalwart in the face of adversity.

Fictional characters can serve to make us aware of social issues, but witnessing the experiences of real itinerants is far more confronting.

In the 1980s, I was on a 24-hour assignment to photograph London dustmen at work. In the early hours of the morning, I watched them clean up in order to maintain the city's veneer for tourists and commuters. In a nightly ritual, a group of itinerants slept under the bridge near Embankment

itinerant

tube station, close to the River Thames. The air was damp and musty. To shield themselves from the cold, they placed flattened cardboard boxes on the pavement. It was an eerie and depressing sight to see the rows of shadowy recumbent figures. In the early dawn, I watched three dustmen rouse these homeless people and dispose of the cardboard before the station opened and the business day began. This all happened within a 25-minute walk from Buckingham Palace. Ironically, George Orwell's memoir, *Down and Out in London and Paris* (1933), mentions homeless people sleeping in that same area 50 years earlier.

Fortunately, most newcomers aren't homeless or sleeping on the streets and, for the majority, our feelings of itinerancy will pass. As newcomers, we lack personal connections and local knowledge, so we have less social standing. People who have had the luxury of remaining in one place can't easily appreciate how a newcomer's ability to survive is, in itself, an important achievement.

Whatever we are called: immigrant, refugee, itinerant or newcomer — our expectations are different because we are just trying to survive.

— Ethel Meadows, teacher

J

journey

noun   an act of travelling from
         one place to another

verb   to travel somewhere

J

We have all met them — well-meaning, hackneyed conversationalists who intone, 'You are on your journey' or 'The journey is never ending.' Affirming our shared, spiritual road trip, they are also congratulating themselves on being one step ahead of us in the quest for enlightenment.

Despite this, the word 'journey' has a respectable pedigree. Books, television programs, films and plays use it as a metaphor to illuminate different perspectives on the art and science of travelling through life. These metaphors can hold special relevance for newcomers.

Jules Vern's science-fiction classic *Journey to the Centre of the Earth* (1864) tells the story of three intrepid explorers who discover dangers deep beneath the earth's core. These characters undertake a literal journey with creative licence.

Eugene O'Neill's *Long Day's Journey into Night* (1942) takes us on an imaginary trip into the American playwright's turbulent past. But journeys are not only for humans. *The Incredible Journey* (1961), a children's novel by Sheila Burnford, follows the adventures of two dogs and a Siamese cat as they cross the Canadian wilderness to reunite with their owners.

'Journey' can also provide instant gravitas for scriptwriters. In the Marvel film *Avengers: Endgame* (2019), superhero Ironman says to his gleaming helmet, 'Part of the journey is the end', admitting his chances of survival are poor. Fortunately, he survives this homily: the Marvel franchise is eager to continue his lucrative return trips to the screen.

For the newcomer, 'journey' is part of our essential vocabulary. When we move, we need to reconcile the dual aspects of our destination: the external (physical) with the internal

journey

(emotional). Our outward journey is complete once the boxes have been unpacked and we have found the nearest pharmacy or train station. Our inward journey, however, does not respond to a schedule and will not necessarily go to plan.

For the newcomer everything is magnified. Small things that are barely discernible to others have a huge impact. As a child, I remember the excitement of a first invitation to a new friend's home and, later, of finally feeling confident enough to invite someone to play at our house. These first invitations, whether to a party or to join a club, can feel life altering. These intense feelings are not exclusive to newcomers, but the difference is that our experience is repeated over and over again with each move.

However, moving can also allow us to escape. As an adult, I decided to move to another city rather than face up to some harsh realities in my personal life, but this only postponed the inevitable day of reckoning.

A journey is a person in itself; no two are alike. And all plans, safeguards, policing and coercion are fruitless. We find after years of struggle that we do not take a trip; a trip takes us.

— John Steinbeck, author
Travels with Charley: In search of America

K

keepsake

noun   anything kept, or given
to be kept, as a token of
friendship or affection;
remembrance

K

Keepsakes are tokens of affection exchanged between lovers, family or friends. This hybrid word emerged in the 18th century to describe an object 'kept for the sake of the giver'. Generally, keepsakes are small and lightweight and may be given on a festive day, an anniversary or special occasion. We might give or receive a decorated book, a miniature photograph or silhouette portrait, a snippet of hair, a knitted scarf, an embroidered handkerchief, a ribbon or locket.

It is understandable why keepsakes became popular in times when life was precarious and average life expectancy was short. Survivors of the deceased took solace in a small possession directly connected to their friend or loved one. For me, keepsakes have sentimental associations with the novelists Jane Austen, Louisa May Alcott and the Brontë sisters: Jane Austen died at the age of 41; Louisa May Alcott, who wrote *Little Women*, lost her sister Elizabeth at the age of 22; and the Brontë family did not fare well either — Emily and Branwell both died in their early thirties, while the youngest sister Anne died at 29.

Mourning jewellery — often a locket, a ring or a brooch in which a snippet of the deceased's hair is encased — was at its most popular during the Victorian era. After the untimely death of her husband Prince Albert at the age of 42, Queen Victoria spent the rest of her life dressed in black and wearing mourning jewellery.

Is the notion of a keepsake outdated or does it have any value for the newcomer? With the rise of contemporary gurus such as Marie Kondo, we are encouraged to declutter our homes and lives. But what is clutter and what is a keepsake?

keepsake

Clutter is merely stuff whereas keepsakes have close associations with people we care about, helping us recall cherished memories. They are tangible reminders of a past that others don't share and, for the newcomer, a reminder of people and places left behind.

To the uninitiated, keepsakes can be mistaken for clutter. Why hang on to that fraying T-shirt, dingy stuffed toy or broken piece of jewellery? Certain objects bring us comfort, but for the newcomer they have added weight, serving as the only remaining evidence of important past relationships or events. Keepsakes might be relegated to the non-essential, but emotionally, they are priceless.

It's easier to die than to move ...
at least for the Other Side
you don't need trunks.

— Wallace Stegner, author
Angle of Repose

L
lost

adjective

1 unable to find one's way; not knowing one's whereabouts

2 that has been taken away or cannot be recovered

lost

For the newcomer, those first few weeks after a move can feel as though we have taken residence in an emotional nether region — lost between yesteryear and the present; existing somewhere between the moon and the planet Mars.

Before getting lost in space was an option, losing your way was a time-honoured tradition in folklore and fiction. Fairy tales caution us of dire consequences should we lose our way. The Brothers Grimm first published 'Hansel and Gretel' in 1812. Abandoned by their mother, two children become lost in the forest. Drawn to the aroma of spicy gingerbread and warm sugary candy, they are lured into the clutches of a wicked witch who wants to eat them for dinner. And in another Grimm story, 'Snow White' (1812), the heroine loses her way and is rescued by the seven dwarfs, only to fall victim to the evil Queen's poisoned apple. This tale inspired Walt Disney's 1937 pioneering animated film.

As a child, I adored the Disney animated adaptation of JM Barrie's *Peter Pan* (1906). Peter's ability to fly and rebellious spirit captured my imagination. I took delight in his companions the Lost Boys and the deliciously scary, ticking crocodile lurking in the waters around the island of Neverland. Peter, we learn, has a keen sense of direction. To travel home, he must fly to 'the second star to the right and straight on till morning'. Peter showed a fearless self-sufficiency and an enviable independence free of adult expectations. A memorable musical version starring Mary Martin premiered on television in 1955. Nimble girls were able to be Peter Pan, too.

With our frequent resettling, to avoid getting lost, my sister and I had to develop navigational skills. She trained

L

herself to use the sun as a compass to determine her location, whereas I used landmarks to find my way. With so many changes in scenery, we became careful observers and I suspect it was this early training that influenced our career paths in the visual arts and photography.

Today's navigational apps for smartphones and cars help us avoid getting physically lost, but our emotions aren't so easily managed. After a move, we might feel that what is lost — close friends, a familiar routine and the comfort of being accepted — can never be regained. However, over time, some missing things will be recovered.

I was lying to myself when I thought I was lost, I have never been lost — I just wasn't ready to be found.

— Nikki Rowe, author

M

milestone

noun

1 a stone set up beside a road to mark the distance in miles to a particular place

2 a significant stage or event in life, history, etc

HAPPINESS
15 MILES

milestone

'Milestone' has an ancient lineage. In the third century, the Romans masterminded a 53 000-mile network of roads and stone markers, known as milestones, across their empire. Since then, the meaning has expanded: milestones herald significant moments in a person's life or signal major transitions such as a graduation, wedding or retirement, setting a firm line between where we have been and where we are headed.

Moving to a new place is like reaching a milestone. It is a chance to pause and reflect on what we have left behind before we take the next step. Defining a move as a milestone recognises its deeper meaning and the subsequent impact it can have.

The impact of frequent moves on our family was never acknowledged. Any problems my sister experienced were discounted. 'Be seen and not heard', was our father's admonishment. We had to accept the inevitable. This acquiescence made things easier for the corporation; we were mere pawns on a business board game. But with these multiple moves came complex feelings of unexpressed loss and powerlessness, and a history that vanished. Our feelings were deemed insignificant, yet each move changed the trajectory of our lives.

The newcomer achieves many minor milestones: the success of getting the internet or television connected; the first invitation to a neighbour's house, or an especially warm welcome at a new club or group.

As newcomers, we can find ourselves in the midst of a complicated emotional transition. Identify this moment as

M a private milestone. Although milestones might seem like hurdles, they can also show us how far we have travelled, measure our progress and, most importantly, give us the impetus to keep going in our new direction.

> With every milestone that I've come across, there's always been a little note at the bottom that's said, Don't worry, there's another milestone coming up.
>
> — Jack Garratt, singer–songwriter

N

newcomer

noun someone who has recently
arrived in a place or
recently become involved
in an activity

N

Newcomers in fantasy and science-fiction stories can be shape shifters, time travellers and alien beings. Fantastic creatures and frightening monsters magically arrive and depart, appear and disappear, at a writer's whim. For my sister and I, at times our lives as serial newcomers felt as though we were living in a weird fantasy story that kept repeating itself, over and over.

Our childhood moves from the southern United States to the north and back again were lessons in state boundaries; we learned to imitate accents and adopt local dress codes. When we transferred from the state of Virginia to Pennsylvania in the north, our southern drawl labelled us as outsiders. We lost the accent. When we first moved to New Jersey, we dressed in conservative girlish clothes with frilly collars while the school's popular girls strode down the hallways in chic, preppy-style outfits, like models from *Teen Vogue*. Assimilating was not about losing our identity, but about assuming a camouflage until we could find our bearings. We quickly learned what to wear and who in the social hierarchy might be friendly.

As perennial outsiders, we had little grasp of how people related to each other, whether as friends or family. We were like aliens from another planet taking part in a social experiment, trying to mimic meaningful relationships that would result in belonging and acceptance.

As we grew older, we could predict that we would be moving again. There was always a sense of urgency as we struggled to find our place before the next transfer. This pressure always made me feel like an interloper disrupting other people's lives.

newcomer

My sister and I turned to reading to help make sense of the world. Many of the characters in our favourite child-hood books had absent parents or were orphans: *The Boxcar Children, Sara Crewe, Pippi Longstocking, Heidi, Madeline, Anne of Green Gables* and *Peter Pan*. Despite being alone, they took risks, sought adventure, respected themselves and others, and achieved happy endings. These were the families we desperately wanted.

Like many of our fictional heroes, my sister and I were forced to accept change, no matter how much we might want to resist. After a move, we faced a confusing array of challenges and choices. Our survival depended on taking direct actions, such as joining the local library or participating in a community activity. But whether we were attending a Girl Scout camp or summer school, it always felt as though we had to pass a test in order to gain permission to live somewhere.

In response, we developed a protective shell to disguise our vulnerability. On the surface, we lived a series of new lives while our true selves remained in a constant state of anxiety, struggling to adapt and find stability.

My favourite books were always
about orphans. I became very secretive.
I became suspicious of everyone.
I became unable to be my real self.

— Lena Horne, singer and actor

O

outsider

noun 1 a person who is
not involved with a
particular group of
people or organisation
or who does not live in
a particular place

2 a person who is not
liked or accepted as a
member of a particular
group, organisation or
society and who feels
different from those
who are

outsider

Moving is different for each of us. Our age, education, ethnicity, family relations, finances, history, personality and interests, together with the size and location of our new community, all have an impact. Despite our differences, newcomers, better than most, share an understanding of what it feels like to be an outsider.

I was entering second grade when we transferred to Pennsylvania. With complications from the move, I was late starting the school year. Mother accompanied me on my first day. We entered the classroom. Children were seated at low tables and there was one seat available so I went to it and sat down.

Mother introduced me, thanked the teacher and as she turned to leave I started to cry. I *never* cried, but this room full of strangers and their curious stares overwhelmed me. Flustered, she assured the teacher that normally I didn't behave like this.

We had moved three times in four years and I simply did not have the words to express my distress. From then on, I was branded a crybaby and a problem. At this early age, I learned it was a luxury to express my emotions.

People often take their home, family and friends for granted, but outsiders must work to gain acceptance and to earn their place, despite feeling as though they will never be at home again regardless of how much effort they make.

Feeling like an outsider is not unique to newcomers. Most of us will experience a moment when we feel like an outsider, whether we are starting a new job or joining a club where we don't know anyone. A benefit for newcomers in these situations is that we can choose which aspects of ourselves to

O

reveal. However, skin colour or a visible disability cannot be hidden and leave us open to discrimination or racial vilification.

Outsiders recognise insiders because they exude a confidence that comes from belonging. An outsider can try to be a chameleon — to blend in and avoid detection — or they can choose to turn their difference into an advantage. The Australian performer Steady Eddie (b. 1968), who has cerebral palsy, began his career as a stand-up comedian, forcing his audience to confront their attitudes toward disability.

Whether we feel like a temporary or permanent outsider, our position comes with a heightened awareness of our difference. As keen observers of insiders, we may decide that it is preferable to remain on the outside. In the end, self acceptance is the only way to navigate these feelings.

Professional newcomers can become professional pretenders; we learn to mask our feelings in order to persuade insiders that there isn't any real difference between us and them. But the feeling of being an outsider lingers.

> Always being the outsider, you feel comfortable everywhere, but you don't really feel at home anywhere.
>
> — Ronny Chieng, comedian

P

passage

noun 1 an act or instance of passing from one place, condition, etc to another; transit

2 a portion or section of a written work; a paragraph, verse, etc

3 a phrase or other division of a musical work.

verb to make a passage; cross; pass; voyage

P

The word 'passage' is at its most expressive when used in the phrase a 'rite of passage', signifying a transition into a new phase of life, such as entering adulthood or retiring from work.

For young Australian Aboriginal males, entering adulthood is marked by going walkabout in the bush for up to six months. When Jewish children reach puberty, they have a celebratory event — a bat mitzvah for girls or a bar mitzvah for boys.

To heighten suspense in mystery stories, writers use the time-honoured plot device of a secret passage, hidden behind a bookcase or disguised behind a door. In the evocative novel *Jamaica Inn* (1936) by Daphne du Maurier, the innocent heroine, Mary Yellan, discovers an underground passage used by bloodthirsty smugglers to move illicit goods under the cloak of darkness.

Whether in fact or fiction, secret passages do not necessarily follow a direct route or lead to a safe haven and we might not like what we discover. The ancient Egyptians incorporated them in the pyramids to confuse and entrap tomb robbers. In 16th-century England, the Protestant Queen Elizabeth I persecuted Catholics and outlawed Catholicism. As a result, secret passages and tiny chambers, called 'priest holes' could be found in the homes of sympathisers who would hide priests when authorities came searching.

During the United States Civil War (1861–65), the Underground Railway ferried slaves to freedom with the aid of a network of secret rooms and passages in abolitionist homes. Slaves wrote musical passages — songs with encoded mes-

passage

sages — that they would sing in order to help each other escape to freedom.

Our summers were spent at our grandparents' home outside Gallipolis in the Ohio countryside. My sister would find places to hide and read. She would climb up a sycamore tree with her book, some cheese and an apple, and spend the day reading. Sometimes she climbed out the window on the stair landing and onto the metal roof. But her favourite place was the highest shelf in our grandparents' bedroom closet. She would turn on the closet light, shut the door, and read undisturbed for hours. No one ever found her there. It was her own priest hole.

A move can be confronting: it feels as though we are undergoing a rite of passage *and* entering a secret passage. We take our tentative first steps, prepared for unexpected twists, turns and mysterious encounters with strangers.

Passages can materialise exposing a
hidden world that was there all along.

— Bryant McGill, author

Q

quest

noun   1   a long search for
             something that is
             difficult to find

         2   a quest for the meaning
             of life

quest

For me, 'quest' is the most magical word in this dictionary, conjuring up images of medieval castles, stone parapets, courtly knights in shining suits of armour and chaste maidens wearing conical headdresses, chafing at the restrictions of being the fair sex.

So why does 'quest' matter to the newcomer? Admittedly, we aren't marching to find a Holy Grail and we are unlikely to be wearing armour anytime soon, but we are charging forward, valiantly trying to make sense of our new environment. Along with practical challenges, we attempt to decipher the behaviour of the local inhabitants and understand their culture. A fundamental part of our quest is to find a sense of belonging, of feeling at home.

On a small scale, that quest is different for each of us: it might be finding a local coffee shop where we feel comfortable or pursuing a passion by learning something new, such as how to figure skate or cook Indian food. Some quests will be life-altering, such as a decision to become an artist or to pursue a religious vocation. But we aren't characters in an Arthurian legend and, inevitably, there will be times of uncertainty and confusion.

After a move, the absence of routines and the refuge of close friends can amplify unresolved personal issues, leaving families and individuals vulnerable to suppressed problems.

Making new friends was always a challenge: as teenagers, my sister and I didn't know anyone well enough to confide in about our parents' continuing marital problems, so we rarely felt comfortable enough to bring anyone home to such an unwelcoming environment. Consequently, as an adult, one

Q

of my personal quests has been to have a peaceful and loving home.

Quest is a wonderful word to inspire the imagination. As a newcomer, a move can be the catalyst for a self-styled adventure. If we lack confidence, we can imagine that this quest will be personally tailored to our special talents and abilities.

You didn't get the quest you wanted, you got the one you could do.

— Lev Grossman, author
The Magician King

R

refugee

noun   one who flees, especially
one who flees their country
to escape danger or
persecution

refugee

Refugees existed long before the word was invented. The first group of displaced people was recorded in 74 BC, when the tribes of Israel were expelled after being conquered by the Assyrians.

The word 'refugee' is derived from the Old French *réfugié*, specifically used for the Protestant Huguenots fleeing Catholic persecution in the 18th century. It is a poignant reminder of the Huguenot ancestors on our father's side who became refugees, crossing the Atlantic Ocean to make a home in the New World. On our mother's side, we are descendants of Native Americans who suffered forced exile on the infamous Trail of Tears (1836–39). Persecution, violence and displacement are as much a part of our family legacy as our Huguenot ancestors' sacrifice and dreams for a better life.

Today, the number of refugees in the world is far greater than at any other time in history. In 2020, there were more than 82.4 million forcibly displaced people fleeing for many reasons including religious persecution, political upheaval, conflict, hunger, economics, climate change, sex discrimination and homophobia.[4]

Refugees are also newcomers, but their experience is radically different from ours. When we were growing up, my sister and I were privileged. We lived in clean houses, food was plentiful and the water safe to drink. We had access to good medical care and excellent public schools. Our father had steady employment, we could choose where to worship, and

---

4   United Nations High Commissioner for Refugees (2020) 'Figures at a glance', https://www.unhcr.org/figures-at-a-glance.html, accessed 23 December 2021.

R

we were governed by a stable government. We might have felt isolated, even ostracised, but we were never denied our basic human rights. Although we were never sure of being welcomed, we never felt that our family was in any danger.

If my French ancestors and I were to meet today, they would be incredulous at my higher education, aghast at my belief in women's rights and horrified at my disinterest in formal religion. My freedom of choice has only been possible because of their sacrifices — an enduring gift.

I urge you to celebrate the extraordinary courage and contributions of refugees past and present.

— Kofi Annan, Secretary-General United Nations, 1997–2006

S

sojourner

noun   a temporary resident;
a stranger or traveller
who dwells in a place
for a time

S

The word 'sojourner' first gained my attention when I was in high school and learned about the African-American abolitionist and women's rights activist Sojourner Truth (1797–1883), a former slave who preached the principles of abolition in the United States. Deeply religious, she adopted this descriptive name after being freed. It was a declaration of faith and an unrepentant vow.

Travelling forward a century and a half to the planet Mars, in the late 1990s Sojourner is a robotic miniature rover, programmed to explore this distant planet.

There could hardly be any greater emotional or metaphorical distance between these two Sojourners: one a freed slave from the 19th century and the other a robotic space explorer in the 20th. Is there anything they could possibly share beyond their distinctive name?

Sojourner Truth sought to promote equality across race and gender, moving beyond prejudice and hatred in search of a higher truth. Sojourner the robot was launched to propel humanity's knowledge forward, stretching the boundaries of science and technology. Both woman and machine were on journeys of discovery: the woman forging her destiny as a matter of righteous and religious principle; the machine at the service of science and technology.

Names and words shape our sense of ourselves. As newcomers, our present and future are unpredictable. We might never have the opportunity to live on the heroic scale of Sojourner Truth or be part of a space programme exploring the universe, but becoming a sojourner means we are no longer

sojourner

an ordinary traveller. Wherever we reside, even temporarily, the journey and the destination become of far greater value.

I'm not going to die; I'm going home like a shooting star.

— Sojourner Truth, activist

T

transfer

noun   the movement of something or someone from one place, position, etc to another

verb

1   to move someone or something from one place to another

2   to change to a different job, team, place of work or situation, or to make someone do this

T

'Transfer.' The dreaded word. We were being uprooted again.

Years later, I was a talking to a friend and 'military brat' about our childhoods. I looked at her and said, 'Transfer.' We both grimaced. The word triggered painful memories: she grew up in a military family that was required to move from base to base and I was a corporate itinerant. In my father's case, a transfer was not a promotion, but a sideways move when the company needed a mechanical engineer for a special project.

The constant upheaval made my sister and me feel like guests at the Mad Hatter's Tea Party: we kept changing seats to fresh place settings without ever eating. We never felt in control, nor did we ever have the satisfaction of completing anything.

Our first transfer was from Ohio to Florence, Alabama, where we were building a small ranch-style house in a new suburb. When our parents separated, we left abruptly for a six-month stint in Louisville, Kentucky. After they reconciled, we were to move into the new home in Alabama, but my father took a job in Richmond, Virginia. A year later, we were transferred to Pittsburgh, Pennsylvania, where we acquired two pet cats. Then came the transfer to New Jersey. In preparation for this move, and without our knowledge, our cats were taken to the country and dropped off by the side of the road.

In New Jersey, we rented a split-level bright turquoise house with florid coral pink shutters. In a suburban sea of sedate two-storey, red brick houses and beige and brown timber homes, the house screamed 'renters', 'transients' and 'poor'.

transfer

We were the family who wouldn't be around for long, the family who couldn't afford to buy a home.

With so much change, we had little opportunity to understand ourselves or others. My sister's 4th-grade romantic heart was broken when we left Virginia. Then came a period of happiness for her in Pennsylvania until we transferred to New Jersey as teenagers.

This move proved more difficult. Our father hated the daily commute to New York City. Ironically, it was one of our mother's happiest periods. She loved the Big Apple with its theatres and museums and she began teaching English at our local middle school. But then came the next transfer.

By now, my sister had left for college, but for me everything I hoped to achieve evaporated. I had good grades, was active in athletics and planned to work on the Editorial Committee of the school yearbook. In my Senior year, we relocated again to Richmond, Virginia, where I found myself in yet another high school, without friends, history or connections and with nine months until graduation. There was little time or incentive to achieve anything except maintain my grades and attempt to make the best of things.

To make things more complicated, I spoke with a northern accent and I now held liberal attitudes acquired from living close to New York City and nurtured by an outstanding public school education. I vividly remember the din of the city's traffic, the woody smell of roasting chestnuts from street vendor stalls, and people of every age and description talking with different accents on the crowded pavements. It was a city made for strangers.

T

Transferring to Richmond felt like travelling back in time. I was shocked by the casual racism towards Blacks expressed in everyday conversation; the silent segregation within institutions such as affluent country clubs; and downtown Broad Street that was divided by colour — one side for Whites and the other for Blacks. The city has since changed, but at the time it felt as though I had entered an undeclared war zone.

But beneath the strangeness and struggle, my sister and I had figured out independently how to turn a transfer to our advantage. We could reasonably predict a transfer would occur every two to three years, meaning we could simultaneously take on a new identity, leaving behind our mistakes and the people we disliked. With this final transfer, however, I made the conscious decision to not change my identity ever again. I had begun to suspect that this behaviour might have serious emotional consequences.

For those of us who have moved at the behest of a company or the military, a transfer is a harsh, non-negotiable commandment that could cause families serious problems and have lasting consequences.

People get rid of plenty when they move — sometimes they're changing not just places, but personalities.

— Colson Whitehead, author
The Nickel Boys

U

uproot

verb   1   to pull a plant including its roots out of the ground

2   to force to leave an accustomed or native location

uproot

'Uproot' is a poignant word for the newcomer because it comes closer than any other in describing the physical sensation of leaving to move somewhere new.

After a move, we can feel vulnerable and uncertain, like Dorothy in *The Wizard of Oz* film from 1939 (which differs significantly from L Frank Baum's book, *The Wonderful Wizard of Oz*). Dorothy is at home when a tornado hits. She is knocked unconscious and dreams that the house is blown sky-high, finally coming to rest in the Land of Oz.

Dorothy, uprooted, becomes an unwilling newcomer who does not fit in with her new surroundings. She towers over the small inhabitants of Munchkinland and, to make matters worse, she has inadvertently killed a witch. She learns that she must seek out a wizard to return home and, along the way, she befriends the Lion, the Tin Man and the Scarecrow. Eventually, our unlikely heroine passes enough tests of fortitude and makes her way back home to Kansas.

Unfortunately, our destination won't be the Emerald City and making new friends won't be that easy. When we are uprooted, there is an unsettled period when we need family and close friends but, sadly, most are left behind. Online communication can help, but sometimes this results in greater feelings of isolation. The people we left behind are getting on with their lives. They are still deeply invested in relationships and experiences that we can no longer share.

Most friendships won't survive a move. Relationships with friends from work, school and shared activities, such as sports clubs, are easy and enjoyable, but rely on frequent contact. If we are lucky, there will be one or two special friends with whom

U

we have a deeper emotional connection. Despite distance and change, these friendships will endure and might even last a lifetime. But as special as these friends are, they can't always be available so we need to turn to our parents and siblings for support.

After a move, family members might put on a brave front as they grapple with feelings of anxiety and loneliness. Everyone's foundations are shifting and some of us will cope better than others.

Our parents stayed in contact with another family who also moved frequently. Some time later, by coincidence, both families were transferred simultaneously to New Jersey and we reconnected. They had three children: a teenage son and daughter who were about our age and a son in primary school. Their father was slated for higher management and was quickly moving up the corporate ladder. When we learned he had turned down a transfer, we were shocked. This could result in a major career setback and even jeopardise his current job. What was the reason?

Their daughter was seeing a counsellor and her parents were advised that another move would be disastrous for her mental health. She could not face being uprooted again and desperately wanted to stay in New Jersey where she was just beginning to make friends. It took someone outside the family to recognise the danger for her. I remember being surprised that her feelings were being taken so seriously — quite the opposite of my experience with our parents.

Being constantly uprooted can stunt our ability to build and sustain lasting relationships. For the newcomer, who

uproot

has been uprooted again and again, 'home' is not reliant on geography. 'Home' is feeling a sense of belonging and acceptance through shared histories, continuing friendships and other enduring relationships.

Travel does not exist without home ...
if we never return to the place we started,
we would just be wandering, lost. Home is
a reflecting surface, a place to measure our
growth and enrich us after being infused
with the outside world.

— Josh Gates, musician

V

vagabond

noun   a person who has no home
and usually no job, and
who travels from place
to place

vagabond

Like so many English words, 'vagabond' has had a nomadic existence, originating as *vagabundus* in Latin before passing into Old French as *vagabond* and then into English. It shows up in the Bible in the tale of the brothers Cain and Abel. God curses Cain for murdering Abel and condemns him as 'A fugitive and a vagabond shalt thou be in the earth.'

'Vagabond' joined an impressive list of pejorative words for the temporary resident: dosser, gypsy, drifter, fugitive, knockabout, marauder, nomad, itinerant, transient, vagrant, tramp, derelict, beggar, bum, outcast and — my personal favourite — hobo. This term originated in the United States about 1890. Unlike a tramp, who works only when forced, and a bum, who does not work at all, a hobo is a travelling person with a strong work ethic, willing to do menial tasks for shelter, a meal or small payment. However, 'vagabond' has evolved into a less derogatory word. Vagabonds are people who appear carefree and light-hearted, even if impoverished. Nonconformists, they take pride in their lack of responsibility and ambiguous status, choosing to live by their own rules rather than accept the label of 'outcast'.

Fictional vagabonds are depicted as romanticised outsiders, a more palatable image for society. In *The Vagabond* (1910), the French novelist Colette created the character Renée Néré who makes a living as a travelling stage performer, having renounced a bourgeois existence. In Rudolf Frills operetta *The Vagabond King* (1925), the central character is a beggar and poet who triumphs in a classic rags-to-riches story.

The romanticised vagabond is far removed from homeless people today who face a very difficult existence. For

V

newcomers, identifying with the vagabond frees us from the judgements and expectations of others, reminding us to enjoy our own company and to take pleasure in the present — the philosophy of the classic vagabond.

Wealth I ask not, hope nor love,
Nor a friend to know me;
All I ask, the heaven above
And the road below me.

— Robert Louis Stevenson, poet
'The Vagabond'

W

wayfarer

noun   a traveller, especially
on foot

Centuries before the invention of planes, trains and automobiles, the wayfarer walked from place to place, following ancient trails.

The characters in Chaucer's *Canterbury Tales* were medieval wayfarers of a special kind: they were pilgrims who travelled from London to Canterbury, following the route known as the Pilgrims Way.

During the Middle Ages, groups of professional wayfarers brought entertainment and practical services to settled people. In England, wandering minstrels performed in taverns, at market-places and on village greens. They would tell stories, recite poems, sing ballads and perform acrobatic feats. In France and Italy, touring groups of troubadours would sing at royal courts and grand homes of the wealthy.

Then there were journeymen who would knock on doors and offer artisan services such as carpentry or metalwork. These ancient craftsmen observed a code of good conduct and adopted a uniform to avoid being mistaken for tramps or vagabonds.

Wayfarers were also the social media of their day, bringing news and gossip, the latest ideas and word of popular fashions.

It would have been a hard life, constantly living on the road, but in return these wayfarers found freedom and adventure. Whether troubadour, pilgrim or journeyman, with their arrival came connections to the wider world. Newcomers, then, as now, are catalysts heralding change.

wayfarer

Troubadours have always been more important and influential than theologians and bishops.

— Brennan Manning, author
The Ragamuffin Gospel: Good news for the bedraggled, beat-up, and burnt out

X
xenophobia

noun   extreme dislike or fear of
foreigners, their customs
and religions

X

The 19th century saw Sigmund Freud, the father of psycho-analysis, help popularise phobias, including xenophobia, and maladies such as nervous headaches and fainting spells.

Xenophobes are not the same as racists or white suprema-cists: xenophobia is more plausible — it sounds more 'scien-tific', as though describing the symptoms of someone who is allergic to foreigners. Racists, however, believe that race is the determining factor of human traits and capacities and that one race can be deemed superior or inferior to another.

Many writers have explored this dark side of human nature. 'Beauty and the Beast', a Grimm brothers fairy tale, has been retold and adapted for film many times, including Jean Coc-teau's evocative film *La Belle et la Bête* (1946). Belle, a lovely young woman, becomes the prisoner of a fearsome beast who is really an enchanted prince. Her love releases him from the curse. Without her intervention, he would have been doomed to remain the eternal outsider with a monstrous appearance. This story was also popularised by the Disney company in the animated feature *Beauty and the Beast* (1991).

From fairy tales to the American frontier west ... where even cowboys are not safe from xenophobia. Based on the novel by Jack Schaefer, the classic 1953 film *Shane* tells the story of a quiet newcomer, known only by his first name, who hides a dangerous past. He tries to leave his gunslinger days behind, but, tragically, they will follow him into his present. In both stories, the main character is victim to their past actions. Each hopes to find acceptance and a new begin-ning: Shane is forced to forsake his new home and the Prince

xenophobia

is saved through magical intervention, but each has been shaped by the fear and prejudice of others.

For Ellen and me, xenophobia was not just the stuff of fairy tales and fiction: it was a feature of our young lives, particularly during our time in New Jersey. Our father was vocal in his dislike of New York City where he was forced to interact with people of other races and cultures, which posed a constant threat to his insular world view.

Then, in high school, Ellen began dating a boy of Japanese heritage. Our parents forbade her from seeing him and our mother, who shared our father's view, threatened Ellen and said father would 'take a shotgun' to them. Ellen was not so easily intimidated.

Xenophobia and its close associate prejudice show up in unpredictable ways — and not only when newcomers first arrive.

I was in Sydney, talking on the telephone to a woman I had never met when she casually said something stereotypical about Jews and their relationship to money. I was stunned by this anti-Semitic comment and by her assumption that somehow my American accent meant I wouldn't take offence. Without missing a beat, I told her I was Jewish. There was an awkward pause and we ended the conversation.

Being a newcomer sensitises us to other individuals and communities who struggle for acceptance. I have experienced anti-American bias in England and Australia, both socially and in the workplace. This has shown me how prejudice operates and how we become targets for other people's insecurities

X

and senseless fears. And when that prejudice goes unspoken, as is often the case, it makes life even more difficult because it operates covertly to undermine us.

Refugees, asylum seekers and immigrants are our most vulnerable newcomers. Only reason can protect us from other people's irrational fear of difference.

Those who stole and loot from ShopRite in the reprisal attacks of xenophobia in South Africa left the bookshelf untouched. Readers don't steal and thieves don't read.

— Olawale Daniel, philanthropist and blogger

Y

yesteryear

noun last year or the recent past, especially as nostalgically recalled

A common hazard for newcomers is nostalgia for the past or 'yesteryear'. Imagine trying to play a piano with missing keys: no matter how well you play, the sound will never come out right. And so it is for the newcomer: no matter how hard we wish, we can never return to the past.

After we announce plans to move, we enter what I call the Newcomer Twilight Zone — neither here nor there nor anywhere — a waiting game. Meanwhile, we attend the kind but distressing farewell parties and say our final goodbyes. Regardless of whether a move is by choice, we experience a heightened sensitivity as we try to maintain a façade of optimism while struggling with feelings of sadness and loss.

On our return to Australia, my husband and I were welcomed by family and friends, which helped bridge the distance. They offered us temporary housing and, when we were struggling, gave advice and pep talks. Meanwhile, our family and friends overseas gave us crucial emotional support through emails, online chats and telephone calls.

Yesteryear became less about nostalgia. Caring friends from the recent past moved into our present with understanding and empathy, but even they could not erase the strangeness of our circumstances.

For the second time in my long history of moving, I returned to a city to live again. If I had ever fantasised about moving back, this was a sharp reality check. Back in Melbourne, after more than a decade away, things were familiar yet substantially altered. It felt like we were looking at photographs of the past that constantly shifted in and out of focus. People had moved on with their lives. Eventually, we began to

yesteryear

establish ourselves, finding a home and jobs, but it was very difficult and there were many obstacles, some unpredictable and some to be expected.

Had we known how hard it would be, would it have influenced our decision? It might have shifted the timing, but my husband and I both knew on a deeper level it was the right decision. Did we reflect on what we were leaving behind? Yes. We recognised the seriousness of changing our lives once again and accepted the challenges ahead despite the uncertainty.

'Yesteryear' is an enticing trap for the newcomer: it allows us to acknowledge the value of the past, but it can also block our best efforts to deal with the present. What it can never offer, though, is shelter from the present.

I have learned that if you must leave a place that you have lived in and loved and where all your yesterdays are buried deep — leave it any way except a slow way; leave it the fastest way you can. Never turn back and never believe that an hour you remember is a better hour because it is dead.

— Beryl Markham, aviatrix

Z
zircon

noun   a mineral occurring
as prismatic crystals,
typically brown but
sometimes in translucent
forms of gem quality

zircon

'Stick with me and you'll be wearing zircons' was one of our father's catchphrases, along with 'that's how the cookie crumbles'; anything meaningful or valuable will turn out to be fake or it will crumble in your hands so, to avoid disappointment, lower your expectations.

When they were growing up, our parents never moved. Our mother Betty's first major move came when she married our father. She relocated to the small town of Gallipolis, Ohio, where he worked in the family business, Agee & Son Implement Company. Marrying into an established family with a long history, she found a warm welcome and easy entry into the social scene. But this background did not equip them to handle the pressures of life as corporate itinerants.

Their lives became a cycle of transfers. They didn't have the usual foundation of friends and extended family to help them build a life together. Their marriage was full of unexpressed resentment and frustration. It was like living in a building that is constantly on fire — we were always dousing flames, but we could never figure out where the fire had started or why it couldn't be extinguished. The adrenalin of change had become a substitute for intimacy.

Our father's catchphrase about zircons was an admission both to himself and to us that he was living an imitation life, a life without pleasure or satisfaction. He had done the right thing and followed the preordained path as head of the household and main provider, but he did not have the marriage he wanted, the hoped-for sons or a stable home.

Whether or not it was an intended outcome, our family had become modern-day serfs to the Reynolds Metals Company

Z

feudal lord. We had no control over our schooling or our destiny. We were all disposable, along with our friends, homes and pets. Ironically, even after the divorce, our father continued to work for the company. Loyalty can become ingrained and, even if misplaced, it can be a refuge when nothing else makes sense.

Our parents would eventually remarry, and my sister and I would become strangers in their new lives and marriages.

> Just as zircons are counterfeit diamonds,
> so the childhood of a serial newcomer
> turns out to be a counterfeit childhood.
>
> — Ellen Agee Rehfuss, artist

epilogue

Numerous writers offer practical advice on how to plan and prepare for a physical move, giving tips on how to pack boxes, the best way to pay final bills and how to get mail forwarded. Others offer happy-ever-after stories that reveal the emotional and spiritual odysseys of those who decide to shift overseas to find adventure, preferably to an idyllic location in Italy, France or Britain. We try to sympathise with the challenges of renovating an ancient Roman bath or understand the advice on how best to irrigate the terraced vegetable garden of a French chateau.

Then there are the many television series about international moves, highlighting the added complications of learning a new language, foreign currency conversion rates and the discovery of idiosyncrasies such as most city apartments have only one bathroom. In an English television series about people making the move to a rural setting, it seems the bigger the house hunter's budget, the more difficult it is to find a property that satisfies them; whereas the people with a smaller budget show enormous excitement and gratitude when the host finds a property that has charm and falls within their price range. It is fascinating to see how many people expect this relocation will help them realise long-held dreams.

With all of these newcomer adventures and advice, I kept wondering where I could find a list of tips to help manage our feelings before and after a move. There are some outstanding books and websites (see Resources, page 119) that explore the impact on children, individuals and families who move frequently, but for me there was still something missing.

epilogue

I had always felt awkward sharing my newcomer experience and was deeply suspicious of the proliferation of confessional storytellers. I also felt hampered by the inadequate vocabulary to describe my feelings. Our topsy-turvy childhood had left me with a sense of powerlessness and loss and I found myself not wanting to express these emotions again because it made me feel vulnerable. I had had enough of that growing up.

But then I realised there was a parallel story: an outsider's history full of myths, fairy tales and stories chronicled in the films, television programs and books that my sister and I had enjoyed as children and teenagers, then later as adults. Through this filter, I could explore our peripatetic childhood and finally document those experiences. We had accidentally mastered a shared vocabulary — through fiction and reality — that provided the foundation for this dictionary; a testament to what we had experienced, how we felt, what was lost and what remains.

After six years back in Australia, things are slowly beginning to make sense. My husband and I moved to a small rural town on the outskirts of Melbourne. The town has solid, red-brick churches with bell towers and a stately public school built more than a century ago. Cows and sheep graze on the manicured green hills that surround the town and, being in a mountainous region, we witness dramatic cloudscapes worthy of a painting by Turner or Tiepolo. We own a small Federation-style house that is about a hundred years old, situated on a road that leads out of town. Thanks to my husband's efforts, our garden is abundant with fragrant daphne, pale pink jasmine and protea that are like colourful feathered nests.

epilogue

It was a sunny day when we moved in and a young woman with a baby stroller stopped by the front gate. We introduced ourselves and chatted. She mentioned that her grandfather had helped build our house. It was astonishing to me that a casual passer-by had a direct connection with our new home. There is a solidness to this place — a sense of beauty and continuity that I find both reassuring and hopeful.

I come back to the question my counsellor once posed, 'Now, how do you *really* feel?' Do I finally feel at home? I can never give a definitive answer to this. As a recovering newcomer, I am not even sure I know what it feels like to be completely at home. It is a work in progress. I expect my life to be one of emotional unevenness with recurring insecurities that will surface from time to time.

As I look through the front window of my office at the thick palm tree with its fronds reaching to the sky and bookended by two large maple trees, I realise that being transplanted means you can learn to adapt and flourish. There is an ease and comfort here that comes close to 'being at home'.

In my newcomer way, I am able to belong.

bibliography

Allen, W (21 November 1977) 'The Condemned', *New Yorker Magazine*, www.NewYorker.com/magazine/1977/11/21/the-condemned, accessed 23 December 2021.

Bachman, R (1985) *Thinner*, Hodder & Stoughton, London.

Daniel, O (n.d.) *Goodreads*, https://www.goodreads.com/author/quotes/15221159, accessed 23 December 2021.

Davidson, N (22 January 1998) 'Koontz Exorcises the "Phantoms" Within', *Hollywood.com*, http://web.tiscalinet.it/luigiurato/interv/hollywood.htm, accessed 23 December 2021.

Einstein, A (5 February 1930) to his son Eduard Einstein (Archival Call Number 75990).

Gates, J (2011) *Destination Truth: Memoirs of a monster hunter*, Gallery Books, New York.

Grossman, L (2011) *The Magician King: A novel*, Penguin Books, New York.

Isaacson, W (2007) *Einstein: His life and universe*, Simon & Schuster, Inc, New York.

Janouch, G (1968) *Conversations with Kafka*, S Fischer Verlag GMBH, Frankfurt.

Kamei, M (27 March 2020) 'I'm going home like a shooting star', Sojourner Truth and Motherhood, *Editors Choice Blog*. Adam Matthew Publishing Company, https://www.amdigital.co.uk/about/blog/item/sojourner-truth-i-am-not-going-to-die-i-m-going-home-like-a-shooting-star, accessed 23 December 2021.

King, S – *see* Bachman, R

Krebs, A (1977) 'Groucho Marx, comedian, dead; movie star and TV host was 86', *New York Times*, https://www.nytimes.com/1977/08/20/archives/groucho-marx-comedian-dead-movie-star-and-tv-host-was-86-master-of.html, accessed 23 December 2021.

bibliography

Lacey, S (25 November 1996) *Lena Horne: In her own words*, American Masters, PBS.

Manning, B (2005) *The Ragamuffin Gospel: Good news for the bedraggled, beat-up, and burnt out*, Penguin Random House, New York.

Markham, B (1942) *West with the Night*, Virago Press, London.

McGill, B (4 September 2018) 'Critical thinking, and how to get the respect you deserve', *McGill Media*, https://bryantmcgill.com/passages/changing-mind-move-unnoticed-finding-always/, accessed 23 December 2021.

NME Blog (4 February 2016) 'Watch Jack Garratt's Track-ey-Track on Debut Album "Phase" — Part 1'. *NME*, https://www.nme.com/blogs/nme-blogs/watch-jack-garratts-track-by-track-on-debut-album-phase-part-1-11403, accessed 23 December 2021.

North KE, Martin LJ & Crawford MH (2000) 'The origins of the Irish travellers and the genetic structure of Ireland', *Annals of Human Biology*, 27(5):453−65.

Ovid (12−13 AD) *Epistulae ex Ponto*, IV.9.41 [*Letters from the Black Sea*, book 4, poem 9, line 41].

Robinson, G (24 April 2018) ' "Disobedience" Director Works at Border of "Duty vs Desire" '. *The New York Jewish Week*, https://jewishweek.timesofisrael.com/disobedience-director-tests-boundaries-of-duty-vs-desire/, accessed 23 December 2021.

Rowe, N (18 October 2020) *Passport Symphony*, https://passportsymphony.com/inspiring-wanderlust-quotes/, accessed 23 December 2021.

Stegner, W (1971) *Angel of Repose*, Knopf Doubleday Publishing Group, New York.

bibliography

Steinbeck, J (1962) *Travels with Charley: In search of America*, Viking Books, New York.

Stevenson, RL (1896) *Songs of Travel and Other Verses*, Chatto & Windus, London.

United Nations High Commissioner for Refugees (2020) 'Figures at a glance', https://www.unhcr.org/figures-at-a-glance.html, accessed 23 December 2021.

United States Holocaust Memorial Museum, Washington DC, 'Documenting numbers of victims of the holocaust and Nazi persecution', https://encyclopedia.ushmm.org/content/en/article/documenting-numbers-of-victims-of-the-holocaust-and-nazi-persecution, accessed 23 December 2021.

Whitehead, C (2019) *The Nickel Boys*, Doubleday, New York.

bibliography

Permissions

Excerpt from *Thinner* by Stephen King writing as Richard Bachman. Copyright © 1984 by Richard Bachman. Reprinted with the permission of Gallery, a division of Simon & Schuster, Inc. All rights reserved.

Excerpt from *Destination Truth: Memoirs of a monster hunter* by Josh Gates. Copyright © 2011 by Universal City Studio Productions, LLP. Reprinted with the permission of Gallery, a division of Simon & Schuster, Inc. All rights reserved.

Excerpt from *The Magician King: A novel* by Lev Grossman, copyright © 2011 by Lev Grossman. Used by permission of Penguin Books, an imprint of Penguin Publishing Group, a division of Penguin Random House LLC. All rights reserved.

Excerpt from *Einstein: His life and universe* by Walter Isaacson. Copyright © 2007 by Walter Isaacson. Reprinted with the permission of Simon & Schuster, Inc. All rights reserved.

Excerpt from *Conversations with Kafka* by Gustav Janouch, translated by Goronwy Rees, copyright © 1968 by S Fischer Verlag GMBH, translation copyright © 1971 S Fischer Verlag GMBH. Reprinted by permission of New Directions Publishing Corp.

Excerpt from *The Ragamuffin Gospel: Good news for the bedraggled, beat-up, and burnt out* by Brennan Manning, copyright © 1990, 2000, 2005 by Brennan Manning. Used by permission of WaterBrook Multnomah, an imprint of Random House, a division of Penguin Random House LLC. All rights reserved.

Excerpt from *Angle of Repose* by Wallace Stegner, copyright © 1971 by Wallace Stegner. Used by permission of Doubleday, an imprint of the Knopf Doubleday Publishing Group, a division of Penguin Random House LLC. All rights reserved.

Excerpt from *Travels with Charley: In search of America* by John Steinbeck, copyright © 1961, 1962 by The Curtis Publishing Co; copyright © 1962 by John Steinbeck; copyright renewed © 1989, 1990 by Elaine Steinbeck, Tom Steinbeck and John Steinbeck IV. Used by permission of Viking Books, an imprint of Penguin Publishing Group, a division of Penguin Random House LLC. All rights reserved.

Excerpt from *The Nickel Boys: A novel* (winner 2020 Pulitzer Prize for Fiction) by Colson Whitehead, copyright © 2019 by Colson Whitehead. Used by permission of Doubleday, an imprint of the Knopf Doubleday Publishing Group, a division of Penguin Random House LLC. All rights reserved.

resources

Key search words

alien
asylum seeker
culture shock
dual citizen
dual national
émigré
emigrant
emigration
expat
expatriate
expatriation
home
homeland
homesick
immigrant
immigration

long distance
migrant
migration
moving
moving day
moving house
PCS/Permanent Change
    of Station (military)
relocation
repat
repatriation
transit
transition
wanderer
Xpat

Books

Asterisked titles provide exhaustive reading lists or links to relevant websites.

Boehm, SE (2015) *The Essential Moving Guide*, Essential Engagement Services, Los Angeles

Janssen, LA (2013) *The Emotionally Resilient Expat: Engage, adapt and thrive across cultures*, Summertime Publishing, Stamford, England*

Lemieux, D & Parker A (2013) *A Mobile Life: A new approach to moving anywhere*, Xpat Media, The Hague*

resources

Internet

Bologna, C (27 June 2018) 'What Happens to Your Mind and Body When You Feel Homesick', *Huffpost*, https://www.huffpost.com/entry/what-happens-mind-body homesick_n_5b201ebde4b09d7a3d77eee1, accessed 23 December 2021

Horne, L (co-author) (1 May 2021) 'How to Cope with the Stress of Moving', *Wikihow.com*, https://www.wikihow.com/Cope-With-the-Stress-of-Moving, accessed 23 December 2021

https://www.expatica.com

expatinfodesk.com

expatforum.com

biographies

Joyce Agee had already moved home seven times with her family, up and down the east coast of the United States, by the time she entered college. As an adult, she lived in England, Australia and the United States, pursuing a career as a freelance photographer and exhi- bition curator, working in the arts and

cultural sectors of local government and higher education. In 2014, after a fifteen-year stint in Seattle, Washington, Joyce and her husband returned to Melbourne, Australia. It was there that she began to write *The Newcomer's Dictionary* as an exploration of the feelings that had arisen from a life- time of arrivals and departures.

Ellen Agee knew by the age of five that she would be an artist. She is drawn to mixed media and installation work, and has a Master of Fine Arts in Fibers from Southern Illinois Uni- versity. Her most recent exhibition, 'The Law School Brain', is a series of glass mosaic brains, inspired by her studies at Seattle University School of Law.

Made in the USA
Las Vegas, NV
01 July 2022

50947744R00077